LAPSES & ABSENCES

SELECTED POEMS

TOBI COGSWELL

Blue Horse Press
PO Box 7000-148
Redondo Beach, CA 90277-8710

Cover Photo: *Abandoned Station, Aberdeen, Maryland* by Jeffrey C. Alfier

Editor: Bryan Roth

Author Photo: gabrielle

ISBN 978-0615923734

These poems are collected from five previous chapbooks and one full-length collection, sometimes in a slightly different form, as follows:

Sanity Among the Wildflowers (2005): Cello; Redemption; Deaf Escape; Lapses & Absences

Hostage Negotiation in Negative Land (2006): Forfeited; What I Know; Camouflage; Parking Lot Prayer

Carpeting the Stones (2008): Blue-Gray Door; Carpeting the Stones; Sad Kings and Sideways Fishes; Jumping the Constellations; All She Can Do

Poste Restante (2009): The Ripening; General Delivery; The Road Sung South; At the Country House One Sunday in Provence; Eating Baby Artichokes at *Il Bacco Felice*

Surface Effects in Winter Wind (2011): In the Dark, in the Rain, the Night; Surface Effects in Winter Wind; Possession Sound, Whidbey Island, Washington; Bourbon Street Insomnia; Be in Their Memories; The Boy at Cannon Beach; Wrapped in Nothing; Brunch

Lit Up (2012): Two Gentlemen Discussing Beauty by Mail; Applewood Bridge in August; Wish You Were Here; A Lure and a Memory; The Man Checks His Calendar and Schedules Contentment; Drought

Winds

Brass

Strings

Percussion

Jeffrey and Owen

Always. In any language, any weather, with any music playing in the background.

Wish You Were Here

An outdoor taverna in Oia,
the sunset a postcard cliché.

Campari in an old juice tumbler for me.
You, ouzo cloudy in the glass.

The wine you kiss me with,
your mouth a vessel of oceans and time.

The nape of my neck, your arms around my waist.
The way we hold each other still.

Kiss me again.

Lapses & Absences

She takes her heart out,
holds it in her palms.
She can still draw breath,
the heart defending her
but not defining her.
She feels like the heron
landing on a perfect lake,
with perfect light, no language
to speak of, just being.

She looks in wonder at it
beating there, palms up
in holy supplication.
She can only see the hint of hands
beneath her fragile insides
turned and laid bare.

She has loved. She is lost.
She cannot bear to acknowledge grief,
rage with anger, or tally up the losses;
she merely holds her heart with perfect posture
out of curiosity and defense,
the missing part of her soul
holding her close.

And so she flies, her migration
on the wind. She always
threatened to escape.
She wears her bruises
like beauty marks
but does not acknowledge them.
Absence merely means presence
somewhere else, and home
can be anywhere.

The Ripening

It is summer. You are fifty
going on twenty, she is your girl
next door. She invents the words
you want to say, laughs
as she climbs a tree, dares you
to come get her, move in
close and hold her—

her hair wild like blackberry brambles
offering themselves and their fruit,
her kiss sweet as tea.
Wild and sweet, bare knees
and skinned elbows, she reaches
her arms around your neck, pulls
you toward her.

That secret place—you go back
again and again.
That luminous wind
and the mockingbird.
Your voice. Her voice.

In the Dark, in the Rain, the Night

Light the fire and open a window,
smell the smoke mixed with earth,
mixed with red, mixed with blood.

Rain glimmers the lights like a Hockney
print. When the power goes out
the silence takes us back.

Remembered art leaves us
to our own harmonies. I hear all
the words you do not say.

Wrap your leg over mine, I need more
heat. First open the Merlot.
Pour just one glass by the only candle

we can find. I want you near me.
In this quiet of the dark
I crave to learn you.

The music of everything you are
beats a powerful concerto,
rich in woodwinds and brass.

Stand and take a bow,
you are the only one
with a solo this evening.

Sad Kings and Sideways Fishes

Today you drove an hour
to tell me I look pretty
in the sun and to look
at my collages.

When the scent of the sea
engulfs everything with briny prickliness,
thistles jabbing and the water dark
as secrets, I wonder about the canvas
on the far side of respectability,
where colors and images
make wonderful stories

about sad kings and sideways fishes,
goblets filled with salt and stone,
where giant lips touch themselves
to the temples of believers.
The whole is tied down
to keep still in the wind.
I am waiting, spinning
fantastical comedies
with multiple hues.

Tonight I smelled smoke,
the candles from dinner
and the wine mottling our faces—
sad kings and sideways fishes
relegated to the time between
dawn and day.

Blue-Gray Door

How far does he lean
over the precipice?
When he wakes
and grabs at the lifeline
of vine and ivy above,
who will be left
shell-shocked and bitten,
dashed in space?

How many secrets
are one too many,
shadows telling of moss-scented
shells, wine, words that bring
gryphons to their knees?
What bears repeating
behind the blue-gray door?

Windows clouded and yea high,
the cracked symmetry
of sturdy boards—
no one can rescue the unseen,
though life and all living
is written in the lines, as if

the face of the storyteller
wove such aching fables,
you can almost believe
people were meant to be
broken.

All She Can Do

Her tongue curls as if tasting hot chocolate.
She can't make you feel wanted—
all she can do is kiss you sometimes.

She might whisk the stars to make you look,
but cannot help the clouds that shield her.
She stands at the fire to keep you warm,
ice crystals glisten as they fall at her feet.

The wind on the waves foams,
the smell hits the back of your throat.
The water is black, you can only imagine
the life beneath. You want to float
in her arms, watch as the nouns
she's forgotten fly to the angels.

The moon a neon sign of lonely, she
wonders if you are thinking of her.
She can still write the words to make you blush,
but all she does is kiss you sometimes.
And now it is so cold, she opens
her coat for you to step inside…

The Man Checks His Calendar
and Schedules Contentment

May I come see you this Thursday?
I want to see your toes peeping beneath
your black shoes, and your collarbones.

Watch diamonds winking from your ears,
your short hair pushed back, trace the line
of your jaw with my finger, then kiss it.

Let's have tea, then unfetter the wine.
I am poor in terms of funds,
but wealthy in love. I will bring

a small bottle, enough for one glass each.
Let's toast the quiet beauty of escape,
our free hands poised softly on the table.

Turn around, let me trace the zipper
of your dress to the back of your neck,
where small hairs whorl. I want to bask

in the hush of you. Let us butter some bread
and have civilized conversation. I want
to see you this Thursday. I know there is time.

General Delivery

I touch your lips,
brush your brow. You, wizard
of the terrorizing night, say "breathe,
focus on the pain, breathe—
it will lessen, be more manageable."

I note the red inside
your cupboards, close my eyes.
Behind my lids the piercing shriek
of glass reflecting sun.
A thousand fireworks explode,
I want to run and shatter
the window, but the prism
of your face holds me still.

Make me remember to forget.
I am unsure and I am frightened.
You are a lover of the dark.
I, on the other hand,
bend toward the light.
I do not know if I can be
persuaded to stay
in the in-between.

Parking Lot Prayer

Let me take that cart from you,
you look like you could use help.
Is that sparkle reflecting the city lights
or is that all you, centered and shiny.
You look like so much fun to love.

Let me touch your face, the braille
of you strapped onto fingertips
wishing to know you. Tilt your cheek
into my palm, speak in multi-syllables
the words for thank you. I am the coarse hand
of the stranger you turn to.

Let me ease your burdens.
Your effervescence bubbling
like a flute of champagne
the color of a run in a rose stocking,
one glass perched on the windowsill
becoming a cathedral on blank walls.
You deserve it.

Explosions of the scent you exhale
when kissed, roll forward on a tide
of sea foam and sin.
Let me take that from you.
Let me take that
from you.
Let me take it all from you.

Bourbon Street Insomnia

Three a.m. is your witching hour,
approaching like a lover's train—
too fast and too hard to hang onto.
Put your hand to the screen,
order a drink.

Think about the many things
you've done wrong, the one
thing you've done right. Think
about the flaws you love in strange women
who refuse to look you in the eye.

Think about yesterday's overblown roses
fluttering like flags of surrender
before you lay yourself down.
The terror of nightmares
will make you pay for this
time and again. How are you going
to explain this to anyone?

Grind bottle caps into your shoes,
tap yourself gone. The restless trumpet
and drunken sax say goodnight,
but not goodbye.

Don't think anymore—it's overrated.
Let 3:00 become 4:00,
then become 5:00. Let sorrows
become sighs, the howls
of wretched night turning sweet
as you chew, your tongue
thick with sugar, as you bless
yourself home.

Wrapped in Nothing

She stayed in bed on Wednesday,
listened to the blades of a red
Coast Guard helicopter beat
the wind. The air billowed
around it like when the two of you skipped
stones on the lake, cowards on a quest
for normal rather than face each other,
eye to eye, to find out what was wrong.

Tired sheets a country-western song of lonely.
They do not take the place
of the sweetest times. Nor do they
take the place of the sizzling times,
ice cold beer on sweat-fired
skin, the air around you whirring
to make room for lush sublime.

She used to kiss the back of your neck
while you slept. You always wore a shirt,
because even from the beginning,
you were ready to run. And you did.

Now she is alone. It is a workday.
Her lifeline and love line are both long,
while yours appear lonely and shamed.
She turns away from where your kisses
used to greet her, thinks she will become
like the houses she sees in coffee table books,
stunning red doors and lace curtains,
with nothing inside.

A Lure and a Memory

Stay out of the wine aisle, Inez.
You've plenty, and there's no room
in the pantry for the oatmeal.

Shun the screw tops and corks.
Ignore the tempting languages,
Day of the Dead engravings,

labels with ghostly pines,
and red pickup trucks.
Oh, no Inez, this is no way

to reclaim your youth,
you have a little one at home.
Bright colors and blood-dark

memories—you have no time
for the impulsiveness of temptation.

Redemption

I cannot fasten your necklace, dear wife.
My fingers once straight and purposeful,
are now bent, like the failed branches
of bare winter trees.
I know how they would feel
if they were men.

I touch my fingertips together,
wonder when the feeling left.
I can't remember the last time
you lifted your hair, allowing me

to circle your neck with diamonds,
tiny blonde curls underneath,
bending to the pressure of the chain,
my fingers on the clasp.

Come drive with me to ease my mind.
Let's turn circles in the parking garage
of the train station, make up stories
about the passengers.

Today my love, you drive.
My arm lounges out the window,
waving lazily.

The wind teases
my fingers into chords
I used to play on my guitar,
while I watch your face,
and whisper remembered melodies.

Surface Effects in Winter Wind

Rain on the way, the weary sky,
bored horses and the little boy
wait for the deluge, resignation
and patience in their postures.

I am ruined, kiss me raw
as gales, your fingers
locked gently as we pose,
watching unwieldy
crows chasing a hawk.

The camera set up on driftwood,
on miracles, wind in our hair,
sea miming the colors of sky
at this hour.

You wake from a dream
of strangers and fighter jets
crisscrossing shorelines
of clutter and greed.
You don't know who you are.

Grounded by linens and down,
becalmed and unshaken,
the time of all clocks ticking
in your unbound heart.

Camouflage

Our hiking boots have red laces.
Mine, because I want to look young.
Yours, because you are an artist
making a statement against
the browns, the greens, the grays.

We crunch large leaves together,
leave jagged mosaics behind
to be blown the ways of the wind—
the shattering of another season.

Your women friends are beautiful.
I am the hushed one who waits
and answers when spoken to.
Our red strides match but we do not
touch. You are afraid of me.
It is complicated, yet uncomplicated.

Our lives expand exquisitely
and geometrically to include each other,
but the clock berates us in this undertaking.
We shrug and walk, but do not talk.
We check our watches.

The trees hang leaves
that look like teardrops falling
from masks, hiding their souls
within a camouflage much the same
as our quiet walks hide our fright.

Jumping the Constellations

Hand over hand in a blue-moon sky
I pull myself onto the tail of a comet
streaking across the deepening
horizon. What is one plus one, I ask
as I dangle my feet over the rim.

Those looking up can only see history.
They don't see me looking down,
looking for you, reaching
a questioning hand to pull you up.
Come ride with me toward the night.

We smile, hold hands, jump
across the constellations,
across the mountains,
the sky burning
with the brightness of night.

We stop to undo Orion's belt, wiggle
our toes in the Milky Way.
A nursery rhyme of sheer luck
and fireworks flickering,
you touch my face, your fingers
melt onto the planes of my cheeks.
I am a heritage with no name,

part of the two of us combined —
let's use the word "assimilate" —
and do that as we cross
the Continental Divide
to look for ice cream.

I'll have pistachio and you cherry vanilla.
We'll kiss the Italian flag, put wildflowers
in each other's hair. As soon as our comet
meets the approaching sun, we'll hop off
to bodysurf our way onto the pebbled shore.

Dare me to do this.
You know I will.
Come with me.

Brunch

Rain on the roof sounds like bacon sizzling
and I am a whore for sizzling bacon.

The blackened breakers on stormy days smell
like the taste deep in your throat when kissing.

I could not live far from wet sand. My toes
lithe imprints on the mug shot of every

crime novel. Let the wet climb up my denims,
make me remember a reason to get naked, pray

you are handsome there, too. We can make love
miles away with our door open to the sea.

Hurry, before I get confused
and ravage the frying pan.

Eating Baby Artichokes at *Il Bacco Felice*

Lavender and gold thistle
nestled quietly.
The serene face of a Madonna
within robes of pale green.

Protected by thorns, quick
to puncture the curious
and incautious, those who crave
to create chaos out of order.

Nothing more pressing
than toothing toward the heart,
clean and pure,
the thistle crushed.

Melted butter bears
the cherry-drop
of blood-ink dripped
from a still unhumble tongue.

What I Know

I know almost nothing about nothing,
but I know lonely is the dry of your eyes
when the tears have gone to salt lakes,
ribboned and visible by touch only to you.

Sadness is the sound a lonely woman makes
when looking at a small life half begun
and half lived, or unlived.

I know pretty words can be mandolins,
fine strings delivering sweetness.
Ugly words can be crashing trains.
You cringe, shut your eyes,
live in the nightmare.
Even if only brief, it changes you.

I know the scent on the back of your neck
and that it's not for me, a ritual
from fathers to sons to their sons.

Wisdom does not fly naturally
into outstretched arms. You have to listen.
I know almost nothing about nothing,
but I can cradle your darkest burdens
and help you embrace stillness as your path.

Deaf Escape

When I lie on my right side I can only hear
the refrigerator, its gentle hum a dial tone
of white noise. Nestled in that space
between awake and dark, I wait.

You are offended by my closed eyes
and perceived unwillingness to be
your audience, so you pass by.

When I lie on my left side I can hear
the clock ticking. I can hear your step,
and pause for breath. I ponder the stories
locked deep within you, wait to be invited
to the dance, but you do not hear the music.

My great and glowing sadness is not visible
enough to reach you, and in order to hear you
I have turned away. You are offended by my back
to the door, so once again you walk by.

You tinker, and touch my things.
You cut the tops off flowers. Sometimes
I think you will cut my hair.
I must be ever vigilant, but eventually I sleep.
You are nowhere to be found.

Carpeting the Stones

Our apologies linger unspoken.
I no longer remember the origin
of hurt. Please tell me,
which is the way to forgiveness.

I look out the window,
say *Tree, tell me a secret.*
I am half-poised on the brink
of treasure and don't know
which way to turn.

Water rushes across slate,
carpeting the stones,
the colors winking and sly.

Empty is the negative space
between joy and song,
and I feel safe there,
but inside the white noise
of my solitude I miss you.
Tell me the way.

Forfeited

He sang her until she appeared on notes of glass,
fragile, yet brittle as bark. He touched her
discordant hollows in fine sweet surrounds,
contentment not reaching her shaded eyes.

He lost her, sorrow in a minor key,
memories he'd crave even at last breath.
He missed her as clouds miss their grasp of rain—
plumped full, though porous and empty within.

Fear danced on tiptoes treading through the gate.
He knew he could no longer hear. Deaf,
bleeding with the shrapnel of her high notes,
her refrain someone else's song to sing.

Cello

She is reflected backwards
in a shadow box of mirrors,
her head nodding to the beat—

a Scottish love ballad
fine and keening. Her toes,
naked under the lace of her

long dress, tap on the AstroTurf
under the folding chair
from Ace Hardware—an ordinary

reddish-slate chair, cold
to the touch.
She does not have time

to eat, her exercise the hours
of playing beautiful
and solitary music.

No matter if hundreds listen
or no one listens, it is beautiful.

Two Gentlemen Discussing Beauty by Mail

Farm girl beauty is like an old coastal church,
stark to the eye, but strong as wheat grass,
hidden in a field between yellow daisies
and the eyes of those who don't see.

A prairie woman has skin older
than the plains, a peaceful countenance,
a child by the hand and one on her hip.
A smile plays about her sense of hard work.
She is a woman you want to know,
to learn from and love completely.

Broken beauty can go either way.
You can see what she once was,
will never be again. The palm of her hand
on your cheek will tell stories
worth dreaming, a bit crinkled

and worn like bedsheet marks
across the stomach of a lover, not
forgotten when you make your list
of who fulfills your wants.

Shadows of each glow like rekindled flame.
Be careful—they burn.

The Road Sung South

The lengthy road marks a fierce journey—
as birds construct their nests, so she sings on,
weaves a wreath of untamed flowers.
She gathers him close beside her, the lined road
whirring in the heat of nature's handshake.

Long miles can heal the most broken of men,
turned south by the soured expectations
of innocent carpenters who think time
can restore all cracks and blisters.

"Distance!"he cries to the rearview mirror,
his fingers lightly drumming on the dash.
Scent of spring, her skirt is lemon yellow.

Drought

I was the girl behind you
at that stoplight in Laredo.
Your shirt, the dark green color
of waxed magnolia leaves,

long sleeves rolled up, knuckles
at 10 and 2, craggy as mountains
ringing a desert flatland.

You lifted up your sunglasses
and glanced back, eyes dark
as moods with masterful
brows, you tipped your hat
ever so slightly, and hid
them, protected once more.

Your cheekbones could
slice me in two—I wanted
so badly to pull over and give
you that chance.

I have done a lot of things
that crossed the line
from sacred to unholy.
I could have written anthems
of possibility on your reflection
in the rear view. You're why we have church.
You set me on fire, sir,
but when the light changed, I did not follow.

Be in Their Memories

Tired as sin,
reach over the ditch,
pick an apple.
The bicycle seat presses
into your thighs,
skirt hiked up and blowing
in the truck backwash
along the road.

Stop at the winery, drink pink.
Wrap a bottle in a bandana.
Let the sun wash the scent of lavender
across your chest as you drink.

Visit history, eat figs.
Study the texture
of brushstrokes on real paintings.
Gauge the artist's sanity,
how the sounds of the blue
make you want to slap him and cry.
He has the perfect hands,
makes perfect music.

Wear a hat with ribbons.
Take photographs of lovers
with their own cameras.
Leave them
with the only proof
they were ever in the same place at all.

Applewood Bridge in August

We stand on the bridge
in scarletting twilight
and watch the river.
It moves the way you say
my hair looks on the pillow.
I have to believe
that is true and beautiful.

I tell you about
my fifth-grade boyfriend,
who held my hand
on this very same spot.
Windowpane-checked
shirt, bought and buttoned
to the chin by his mother,
chest pocket burgeoning
with skimming stones.

I still remember
his slicked-back hair,
that stupid black comb
all the boys carried,
and his sharp elbows.

You are so much more,
yet I describe you so privately.

We write notes to each other—
sealed in separate jars
and dropped quietly
into the darkening water.
I write mine with invisible ink—
no one else deserves to know
what I know.

Possession Sound, Whidbey Island, Washington

The canyon water ran black,
the driftwood was gray.
Sky blended into sea,
a seamless bone.

Old timber, sharp to the touch,
piled at random
and discovered at the end
of an uneven spider-webbed path.

The lapping of tiny waves announces
a boat. A fisherman, a net, all
the same soft, icy hue.

Light candles, listen
to the drone of seaplanes,
shorebirds hopping with agendas
we cannot know.

You don't have to tell her
you love her. All this gray,
splintered silence, tells her
as if the sea could speak,
and you made this place
just for her.

At the Country House One Sunday in Provence

Pears and honey—
des poires et de miel—
sweetness that transcends
a language meant to know in the bones
as I know in my bones.

When is a glance not a glance,
but a living history, a hand to the cheek,
viens ici, the crust of a bread
cracking the family tree? Salt.
No salt. I can afford to keep you,
or I can't.

Let's have some sugar.
Let me taste from your lips
the things we do not say.

I wear a green dress.
You see my legs through the silk.
They are not frightened, they are
one, two, strong, and standing
in front of you—a dare, not
an acquiescence.

Write me a letter *en français, peut-être
en anglais,* it does not matter. I want
to feel each stroke of your pen
as if a caress.

Des poires et de miel under glass.
An antique table and Mozart in the courtyard —
a window so high, we don't know
if it's someone playing,
or an old-fashioned phonograph.

Gentle the pins from my hair,
your hand finds the back of my neck.
A sweet kiss, another crust of bread.
Let's stir our coffee and grow old.

The Boy at Cannon Beach

for Owen

He wiggles his toes
in a private gully, so far up
the beach there is no kelp
or crab to keep him company.
Old voices of damp and cold
around him are not visible
beneath the sodden sky.
He is always left behind.
The occasional clink
of bottles adds to the jazz
brewing in his head
that comes out as blues.

Three blocks away, the sun
is chatty and conversational,
but here it is stoic as the boy,
offended at being called irresponsible
by a father named for that word.
He walks the punishment
as if it were tattooed on his face.
Where is the music this boy plays,
the graceful sounds that bloom inside.

A lesson in cold-molding, the sand
and boy are hardened by stubborn tides.
Only the ankles to the toes are hidden
in the wet ribbon of stream
on the wide-packed beach. He reaches
down into the water so he can feel
the feet that will carry him, see the hands
that will save him, his own private clock
in his own human time. And so he walks
toward the sun, arms outstretched
in greeting. Damp footprints remind him,
and everyone, that we love the best we can
and then we're gone.

About the Poet

Tobi Cogswell is a multiple Pushcart-nominated poet whose poems have appeared in *The Chaffin Journal*, *Gargoyle*, *Hawai'i Pacific Review*, *The Los Angeles Review*, *Spoon River Poetry Review*, and other print and online journals in the United States and overseas. *Lapses & Absences* is her sixth chapbook. She is also the co-editor of the *San Pedro River Review*. You may contact Tobi at editor@sprreview.com.